Digital Domination:

Mastering Online Reputation and Branding for Unstoppable Business Success

By Brian Carson

Contents

Unlock the Secret to a Stellar Online Reputation and Branding Strategy!

As a business owner or entrepreneur, you know that your online reputation and branding strategy can make or break your success. In today's digital landscape, it's more important than ever to have a strong, consistent online presence that reflects your values, expertise, and achievements. But, let's be honest – managing your online reputation and building a powerful brand presence can be daunting and time-consuming. That's where we come in! Introducing Rep Master, the ultimate online reputation and branding system designed to help businesses like yours thrive in the digital space. Developed by industry experts with years of experience in digital marketing and reputation management, Rep Master provides a comprehensive suite of tools and strategies that can take your online presence to new heights.

With Rep Master, you'll discover how to:

- Build and manage your online reputation effectively, ensuring your business stands out from the competition
- Craft a strong and consistent online brand presence that resonates with your target audience
- Leverage social media platforms to boost your online reputation and enhance your branding efforts
- Handle negative reviews and navigate online reputation crises with confidence
- Measure the success of your online reputation management and

branding initiatives to ensure continuous improvement

But don't just take our word for it! See for yourself how Rep Master can revolutionize your online reputation and branding strategy.

Schedule a Free Demo Today at www.RepMaster.io

By taking the next step and scheduling a demo, you'll gain access to the powerful tools and expert guidance you need to elevate your online reputation and brand presence. Don't miss this opportunity to unlock the secret to a stellar digital presence and skyrocket your business success!

Remember, your online reputation and brand are the keys to your success in the digital world. Don't leave them to chance.

Take action now and experience the transformative power of Rep Master. Visit the URL below to schedule your demo and embark on the journey to a stronger, more impactful online presence.

www.RepMaster.io

We look forward to helping you achieve your digital marketing goals and building a lasting partnership that leads to success.

Sincerely,
Brian Carson
Founder
RepMaster.io

Foreword by Liana Ling, Lead Generation Expert

I'm Liana Ling, the CEO of AdSkills, and I know from personal experience that having a solid online reputation is more important than ever in our digital world. As someone who oversees over 12 million dollars in Facebook ads last year alone, I've seen time and time again how a well-put-together online presence can make a huge difference for businesses and individuals alike. That's why I'm so excited to introduce this all-in-one guide on online reputation and branding, packed with super useful insights and hands-on strategies to help you navigate the digital world like a pro.

In my career, I've come across so many businesses and individuals who have a tough time dealing with online reputation and creating a consistent, strong brand presence. But don't worry, this book has got you covered! It's like your personal roadmap to success, filled with practical advice and tried-and-true strategies. You'll learn everything from making the most of social media to dealing with those pesky negative reviews. This guide is for anyone looking to create, improve, or protect their online reputation and brand.

And guess what? This book even covers the not-so-obvious parts of online reputation management, like figuring out if your branding efforts are paying off and having a plan in case things go sideways. These factors are super important for businesses and individuals to stay ahead of the game in the ever-changing digital world.

In today's cutthroat world, a rock-solid online reputation and brand presence are key to success.

So, whether you're just starting out or already a pro, I encourage you to read this book if you're looking to unleash the full power of your online presence and take your reputation and branding game to the next level.

Preface:

In an era where the internet plays an increasingly significant role in our personal and professional lives, the importance of a strong online reputation and brand cannot be overstated. The digital landscape has transformed the way we interact with one another, share information, and conduct business, making our online presence a crucial component of our overall success. With the wealth of opportunities that the digital world presents, it also brings its share of challenges in terms of managing our reputation and developing a compelling brand.

The primary objective of this book is to serve as a comprehensive guide to navigating the complex world of online reputation and branding. It seeks to provide readers with practical advice, expert insights, and actionable strategies that can be employed to establish, enhance, or protect their online reputation and brand. This book is designed to cater to a wide range of audiences, from seasoned professionals seeking to fine-tune their approach to newcomers who are just beginning their journey in the digital realm.

The chapters within this book cover various aspects of online reputation and branding, including building and managing your online reputation, the key elements of a strong online brand presence, utilizing social media platforms, handling negative reviews and addressing online reputation crises, and measuring the success of your reputation management and branding efforts. Each chapter is structured to provide both theoretical understanding and practical examples, enabling readers to apply the lessons learned to their unique circumstances.

In writing this book, we have drawn upon the expertise of industry professionals, as well as extensive research into the latest trends and best practices in online reputation management and branding. Our aim is to provide readers with a holistic understanding of the subject matter, as well as equip them with the tools and knowledge they need to excel in the digital space.

We sincerely hope that this guide will serve as a valuable resource for those seeking to harness the power of the internet to build a positive and impactful online reputation and brand. With the right approach, determination, and the guidance provided within these pages, we believe that anyone can unlock their full potential in the digital realm and achieve their goals.

Introduction

Introduction to Online Reputation and Branding

The digital revolution has dramatically changed the way we live, work, and interact with one another. In today's interconnected world, our online presence serves as a virtual extension of ourselves, playing a significant role in shaping our personal and professional lives. Consequently, the management of our online reputation and the cultivation of a strong, consistent brand have become more important than ever.

This introductory chapter serves as a foundation for understanding the significance of online reputation and branding, and sets the stage for the in-depth exploration of these topics in subsequent chapters.

The Importance of Online Reputation

Online reputation refers to the perception of an individual or a business in the digital realm, which is shaped by their actions, communications, and the content they share. A positive online reputation can lead to numerous benefits, such as increased trust, credibility, and customer loyalty, while a negative reputation can have detrimental effects on one's personal and professional life.

In today's digital landscape, first impressions are often formed through online interactions, making it essential for businesses and individuals to proactively manage their online reputation. The process of online reputation management (ORM) involves monitoring, addressing, and enhancing the digital footprint of an individual or a business, ensuring that their online presence accurately reflects their values, expertise, and achievements.

The Role of Branding in the Digital World

Branding is the process of developing a unique identity, image, and value proposition for a business or an individual, with the aim of differentiating them from competitors and creating a lasting impression in the minds of their target audience. In the digital realm, branding encompasses various elements, such as visual design, messaging, content creation, and customer interactions, which collectively contribute to the overall perception of the brand.

A strong online brand presence not only helps in attracting and retaining customers but also reinforces the credibility and trustworthiness of a business or an individual. As the digital landscape continues to evolve, businesses and individuals must adapt their branding strategies to remain relevant and resonate with their target audience.

Overview of the Book

This book is designed to provide a comprehensive guide on online reputation and branding, covering a wide range of topics and strategies that are essential for success in the digital world. The chapters within this guide delve into various aspects of ORM and branding, including:

- Building and managing online reputation
- The key elements of a strong online brand presence
- Utilizing social media platforms for ORM and branding
- Handling negative reviews and addressing online reputation crises
- Measuring the success of ORM and branding efforts

Each chapter combines expert insights, practical examples, and actionable strategies to provide readers with a thorough understanding of the subject matter and the tools needed to excel in the digital space.

As we embark on this journey, it is our hope that this book will serve as an invaluable resource for those seeking to harness the power of the internet to build a positive and impactful online reputation and brand.

Chapter 1: **Master the Art of Building and Managing Your Online Reputation: Unlock the Secrets to a Stellar Digital Presence**

How can businesses and individuals effectively build and manage their online reputation?

In today's digital world, online reputation is more important than ever. A strong online reputation can be a powerful asset, while a poor reputation can undermine even the most successful businesses or personal brands. In this chapter, we will delve deeper into strategies for building and managing an effective online reputation for both businesses and individuals.

Assess Your Current Online Presence

Before you can effectively manage your online reputation, you need to understand where you stand. Perform a comprehensive audit of your existing digital footprint, including your website, social media profiles, and any online reviews or articles mentioning you or your business. Identify areas of strength and opportunities for improvement. This initial assessment will serve as a baseline for your ongoing reputation management efforts.

Optimize Your Website

Your website is often the first point of contact with potential customers or clients.

Ensure that it is professionally designed, easy to navigate, and optimized for search engines. Conduct thorough keyword research to determine search volume and find the most relevant terms for your business. Incorporate these keywords into your content, meta titles, and descriptions to improve your search engine rankings and increase visibility.

Include high-quality images and engaging content that showcases your expertise, products, or services. Regularly update your website with fresh content and make sure it is mobile-friendly to cater to the increasing number of users who browse the web on their smartphones and tablets.

In addition to these optimizations, consider showcasing positive customer reviews on every page of your website. But make sure they are always your newest reviews. 85% of consumers think reviews older than 3 months aren't relevant. This strategy can help build trust with potential clients and demonstrate your commitment to providing excellent service. By highlighting your best reviews, you'll enhance your online reputation and encourage potential customers to choose your business over the competition.

By optimizing your website for both user experience and search engine visibility, you'll create a strong foundation for your online reputation management efforts. This well-rounded approach will help your business attract more customers, build trust, and maintain a positive digital presence.

Establish a Strong Social Media Presence with Reputation Marketing

Social media platforms offer a powerful way to connect with your target audience, share valuable content, and showcase your brand personality. Choose the platforms that best align with your target audience and create consistent, engaging content tailored to each platform. Be authentic and interact with your followers, answering questions, and addressing concerns in a timely manner. A well-maintained social media presence can help enhance your online reputation and build trust with your audience.

Incorporating reputation marketing into your social media strategy is essential for reinforcing your online credibility. By highlighting positive customer reviews and testimonials on your social media profiles, you can showcase your commitment to excellent service and build trust with potential clients. Sharing these success stories will demonstrate the value of your products or services and help persuade potential customers to choose your business over the competition.

Additionally, consider integrating review widgets or features that automatically stream your most recent five-star reviews onto your social media pages. This not only saves you time but also ensures that your glowing reviews are consistently displayed across your online platforms, further boosting your online reputation.

By combining a strong social media presence with effective reputation marketing strategies, you'll create a robust online image that attracts new customers and encourages loyalty from your existing client base.

Monitor and Respond to Online Reviews with a Proactive Approach

Online reviews can have a significant impact on your reputation. Monitor review sites like Yelp, Google, and industry-specific platforms, and respond promptly to both positive and negative reviews. Always maintain a professional tone and show your commitment to resolving any issues. Thank your customers for their feedback and take any necessary actions to improve your products or services based on the reviews. To take your online reputation management a step further, consider utilizing a review management system that notifies you every time a new review is posted. This will enable you to stay on top of your online reputation and address customer feedback as soon as it's published. Moreover, such a system can help you proactively request reviews from satisfied customers, thereby increasing the number of positive reviews you receive.

When responding to negative reviews, it's essential to approach the situation with empathy and understanding. Apologize for any inconvenience caused and offer a solution to rectify the issue. In some cases, it may be appropriate to take the conversation offline to resolve the matter privately, while in others, a public response can demonstrate your dedication to customer satisfaction.

By actively monitoring and engaging with online reviews, you'll not only maintain a positive reputation but also gain valuable insights into how you can continually enhance your products or services to better serve your customers.

Share Valuable Content

Sharing high-quality, relevant content is a key way to establish yourself as an expert in your field and build trust with your audience. Create and share blog posts, articles, videos, and other content that demonstrates your knowledge, skills, and experience. Offer solutions to common problems and address frequently asked questions to provide value to your audience and boost your online reputation.

In addition to providing valuable content, consider incorporating user-generated content (UGC) into your strategy. Encourage your audience to share their experiences, testimonials, or success stories with your brand. This not only increases engagement but also helps you build social proof and credibility.

Stay up-to-date with the latest trends and industry news, and share your insights and opinions on these topics. This will position you as a thought leader and a go-to resource for your audience. Also, make sure to diversify your content formats to cater to different preferences and consumption habits. This may include written articles, infographics, podcasts, webinars, or even live streaming events.

Finally, be consistent in your content creation and sharing. Regularly posting valuable content across your online channels will not only reinforce your expertise but also help improve your search engine rankings, making it easier for potential customers to find you online. By sharing valuable content and engaging with your audience, you'll cultivate a strong online reputation that supports your business growth.

Engage with Your Audience

Respond to comments and messages on social media, participate in online forums or groups related to your industry, and actively engage with your audience. This will help create a loyal community of followers and customers who will advocate for your brand. Encourage your satisfied customers to share their positive experiences with others and amplify your online reputation.

Building strong relationships with your audience is key to fostering brand loyalty and turning your customers into brand advocates. Create opportunities for two-way communication and show genuine interest in their thoughts and opinions. Personalize your interactions whenever possible, addressing your audience members by name and acknowledging their specific concerns or experiences.

Consider creating a referral or rewards program to incentivize your existing customers to recommend your business to others. Word-of-mouth marketing remains one of the most powerful tools for building trust and credibility, and a happy customer is more likely to spread the word about your brand.

Additionally, collaborate with influencers or industry experts who share your values and resonate with your target audience. This can help expand your reach, increase your credibility, and strengthen your online reputation. By actively engaging with your audience and fostering brand advocacy, you'll create a supportive community that contributes to the growth and success of your business.

Address Negative Content Proactively

If you encounter negative content online, address it proactively and professionally. If possible, reach out to the person who posted the content and attempt to resolve the issue. Demonstrating your commitment to customer satisfaction can help mitigate the impact of negative content and show that your business is dedicated to continuous improvement.

When handling negative feedback, it's important to remain transparent and open to constructive criticism. Avoid being defensive or dismissive, as this can further harm your reputation. Instead, acknowledge the issue, apologize if necessary, and offer a genuine solution or compensation if appropriate. By taking responsibility and showing empathy, you can turn a potentially damaging situation into an opportunity to strengthen your brand image and showcase your dedication to customer service.

Moreover, use negative feedback as a learning experience to identify areas of your business that may require improvement. Analyze the patterns in the criticisms you receive and implement changes to prevent similar issues from arising in the future. This proactive approach demonstrates your commitment to growth and customer satisfaction, which can ultimately enhance your online reputation.

Finally, encourage your happy customers to leave positive reviews, as this can help counterbalance any negative content and create a more accurate representation of your overall customer experience. A steady stream of positive feedback can minimize the impact of isolated negative comments and reinforce your brand's reputation for excellence.

Leverage Analytics and Tools for Proactive Online Reputation Management

To maintain a positive online reputation, it is crucial to proactively monitor and analyze your digital presence. This involves using a combination of analytics tools, social media monitoring platforms, and review monitoring services to stay informed about any new mentions, reviews, or other content related to your brand.

Invest in analytics tools that can help you track and measure key performance indicators (KPIs) such as website traffic, conversion rates, and user engagement. These insights will allow you to identify trends, uncover areas for improvement, and optimize your digital strategy to better serve your target audience.

Social media monitoring platforms are essential for keeping track of your brand mentions, sentiment, and engagement across various channels. By staying informed about conversations related to your brand, you can promptly respond to comments, answer questions, and address concerns, thus fostering positive relationships with your audience.

In addition to social media, monitor online review platforms like Yelp, Google, and industry-specific sites to stay up-to-date with customer feedback. By consistently tracking reviews, you can identify any recurring issues or patterns, allowing you to address concerns and continuously improve your products or services.

Consider implementing a system that automates the monitoring process, enabling you to receive real-time alerts and notifications whenever your brand is mentioned or reviewed. This will help you stay proactive and ensure that you're always aware of your brand's online reputation.

By leveraging analytics and monitoring tools, you can proactively manage your online reputation and ensure that your brand maintains a positive image in the digital landscape.

In conclusion, effectively building and managing your online reputation requires a combination of proactive measures, consistent engagement with your audience, and ongoing monitoring. By implementing these strategies, both businesses and individuals can create a positive and lasting online presence.

[3 Key Takeaways]

- A strong online reputation is built through a combination of a professional website, engaging social media presence, and sharing valuable content that demonstrates your expertise.
- Actively engage with your audience and address negative content promptly and professionally to maintain a positive reputation.
- Regularly monitor your online presence to identify areas for improvement and stay informed about any new mentions or reviews of your brand.

Chapter 2: Discover the Essential Elements for Crafting a Powerful Online Brand Presence that Stands Out

What are the key elements of a strong online brand presence?

The Power of Consistent Branding

Consistency in branding plays a crucial role in creating a recognizable and memorable brand image. Ensure that your brand's visual elements, such as logo, color scheme, and typography, are consistent across your website, social media profiles, and marketing materials. Additionally, maintaining a consistent tone and style in your content will help reinforce your brand's voice and messaging across various platforms.

The power of consistent branding cannot be overstated, as it serves as the foundation for building trust and recognition among your target audience. By maintaining uniformity in your visual elements and messaging, you create an identity that resonates with consumers and leaves a lasting impression. Let's explore further aspects of consistent branding to help you achieve a strong brand image.

Harmonizing Visual Elements

Beyond the basic visual elements such as logo, color scheme, and typography, consider incorporating additional design aspects like patterns, graphic styles, and imagery. This harmonized approach to design will help create a cohesive brand image that is easily identifiable and stands out in the digital landscape.

Developing a Brand Style Guide

A brand style guide serves as a reference point for your team to ensure consistency in branding across all touchpoints. It should include guidelines on visual elements, tone, and voice, as well as specific examples of how to implement these elements in various contexts. A comprehensive brand style guide will help your team maintain consistency and avoid any confusion or discrepancies in your brand's presentation.

Maintaining a Consistent Brand Voice

Your brand voice is the unique personality and tone that is reflected in your content, be it written or verbal. Identify the core values and characteristics of your brand, and use them as a foundation for developing a distinct brand voice. This voice should be maintained across all communication channels, including social media posts, blog articles, email campaigns, and customer support interactions.

Adapting Consistency Across Platforms

While consistency is key, it's also essential to adapt your branding to the specific requirements of different platforms. For example, each social media platform has its unique format, audience, and content preferences. Adjust your visual elements and messaging to suit each platform's style, while still maintaining the core essence of your brand identity.

In conclusion, consistent branding goes beyond the surface level and delves deep into every aspect of your brand's presentation. By harmonizing your visual elements, developing a brand style guide, maintaining a consistent brand voice, and adapting consistency across platforms, you will create a powerful brand image that leaves a lasting impression on your audience.

Going Beyond the Basics: Crafting a Standout Professional Website

A professional website not only serves as the digital face of your brand but also as a powerful tool for engaging and converting visitors. To create a standout professional website that effectively represents your brand and drives results, it's essential to delve deeper into the various components that make up an exceptional website experience.

User Experience (UX) Design

A well-designed website prioritizes the user experience, ensuring that visitors can easily find the information they're seeking and complete their desired actions with minimal friction. Focus on intuitive navigation, clear page layouts, and fast loading times to create a seamless browsing experience. Additionally, consider incorporating accessibility features to cater to diverse user needs and make your website inclusive for all.

Mobile Responsiveness

With more users accessing websites from mobile devices, it's critical to ensure that your website is fully responsive and adapts seamlessly to various screen sizes. A mobile-responsive website not only enhances the user experience but also improves your website's search engine rankings, as search engines like Google prioritize mobile-friendly sites.

Compelling Content and Storytelling

Your website's content should effectively communicate your brand's unique value proposition and engage visitors with compelling storytelling. Focus on creating concise, informative, and persuasive copy that speaks directly to your target audience's needs and desires. Incorporate storytelling techniques to humanize your brand and forge emotional connections with your audience.

Social Proof and Trust Signals

To build trust and credibility with your website visitors, showcase social proof and trust signals throughout your site. Display customer testimonials, case studies, industry awards, and certifications to demonstrate your expertise and the value you provide to your customers. Additionally, consider integrating trust seals, such as security badges, to reinforce the safety and security of your website.

Regular Updates and Maintenance

A professional website requires ongoing updates and maintenance to remain relevant and effective. Regularly add fresh content, update outdated information, and implement the latest best practices in web design and development to keep your website current and engaging.

In summary, crafting a standout professional website goes beyond aesthetics and basic functionality. By prioritizing user experience, mobile responsiveness, compelling content, social proof, and regular updates, you can create a powerful online presence that sets your brand apart and drives results.

Harnessing the Power of Visuals and Storytelling on Social Media

To create an engaging social media presence that captures the attention of your target audience and fosters meaningful connections, it's essential to utilize the unique strengths of each platform and implement creative content strategies that resonate with your audience.

Emphasize Visual Content

Visual content, such as images, videos, and infographics, tends to perform exceptionally well on social media. Invest in high-quality visuals that effectively communicate your brand message and evoke emotions. Create eye-catching graphics, take behind-the-scenes photos, or produce short videos that showcase your products, services, or brand story in a captivating manner.

Leverage Storytelling and User-Generated Content

Storytelling is a powerful tool for humanizing your brand and fostering emotional connections with your audience. Share the stories behind your products, services, or team members to create a more personal and relatable social media presence. Additionally, encourage your audience to share their own stories and experiences with your brand through user-generated content, which can help build a sense of community and authenticity.

Utilize Platform-Specific Features

Each social media platform offers unique features that can enhance user engagement and promote your content. For example, leverage Instagram Stories, Facebook Live, or Twitter Spaces to share real-time updates or host live events. Utilize LinkedIn's publishing platform to share industry insights or thought leadership pieces. By capitalizing on platform-specific features, you can create a more dynamic and engaging social media presence.

Collaborate with Influencers and Industry Experts

Collaborating with influencers or industry experts can help expand your reach and credibility on social media. Partner with individuals who share your brand values and have a strong connection with your target audience. Collaborations can take various forms, such as sponsored posts, joint webinars, or live Q&A sessions.

Analyze Performance and Optimize Your Strategy

Regularly track and analyze the performance of your social media content to gain insights into what resonates with your audience. Identify trends and patterns in engagement, and use this information to inform and optimize your content strategy. Experiment with different content formats, posting times, and promotional tactics to maximize your social media presence's effectiveness.

In conclusion, creating an engaging social media presence requires a strategic approach that combines captivating visuals, storytelling, platform-specific features, collaborations, and data-driven optimization. By focusing on these aspects, your brand can foster deeper connections with your audience and stand out in the crowded social media landscape.

Delivering Value Through Diverse Content Formats and Topics

To provide valuable content for your audience, it's crucial to diversify your content formats and topics, ensuring that your content remains fresh, engaging, and informative. Cater to different preferences and learning styles by incorporating various content types and addressing a wide range of subjects within your niche.

Exploring Different Content Formats

Experiment with different content formats to appeal to a broader audience and increase engagement. Some popular content formats to consider include:

1. Podcasts: Create an episodic series that offers in-depth discussions, interviews, or industry insights. Podcasts can be a great way to share your expertise while providing an accessible and convenient listening experience for your audience.

2. Webinars: Host live or pre-recorded webinars to provide valuable educational content on specific topics. This interactive format allows you to engage directly with your

audience, answer questions, and build relationships.

3. E-books and whitepapers: Create comprehensive guides or research papers that delve into a specific topic, offering valuable insights and actionable recommendations for your audience.

4. Interactive content: Utilize quizzes, polls, or surveys to engage your audience and gather insights into their preferences, challenges, or opinions.

Diversifying Content Topics

Cover a wide range of topics within your niche to demonstrate your expertise and keep your audience interested. Some approaches to diversify your content topics include:

1. Addressing common challenges: Identify the pain points and challenges faced by your target audience and create content that offers practical solutions and guidance.
2. Sharing industry news and updates: Keep your audience informed about the latest developments in your industry, offering your unique perspective and analysis.
3. Showcasing success stories and case studies: Share stories of how your products or services have helped your customers achieve their goals. This not only builds trust but also provides tangible examples of your expertise in action.
4. Highlighting trends and future predictions: Offer insights into emerging trends and predictions for

the future, positioning your brand as forward-thinking and in tune with the evolving landscape of your industry.

By delivering value through diverse content formats and topics, you can effectively engage and educate your audience, strengthening your online brand presence and positioning yourself as a trusted expert in your field.

The Significance of On-Page and Off-Page SEO for Brand Visibility

Search Engine Optimization (SEO) is a key component of a strong online brand presence, as it helps improve your website's visibility in search engine results pages (SERPs). To achieve higher rankings and drive more organic traffic, it's essential to focus on both on-page and off-page SEO strategies.

On-Page SEO: Optimizing Your Website and Content

On-page SEO refers to the process of optimizing individual web pages and content to rank higher in SERPs and drive more targeted traffic. Some crucial on-page SEO elements include:

1. Keyword research: Identify relevant, high-search volume keywords that your target audience is using to find information, products, or services like yours.
2. Title tags and meta descriptions: Write compelling and keyword-optimized title tags and

meta descriptions for each page on your website. This helps search engines understand the content of your pages and entices users to click on your link in SERPs.

3. Header tags: Use header tags (H1, H2, H3, etc.) to structure your content and make it more accessible for both search engines and users.

4. Image optimization: Optimize images by compressing file sizes, adding descriptive file names, and including alt tags with relevant keywords.

5. Internal linking: Create a well-structured internal linking system to help search engines crawl and index your website more effectively, and to guide users through your content.

Off-Page SEO: Building Authority and Trust

Off-page SEO involves activities that occur outside of your website, aiming to improve your site's authority, trustworthiness, and online reputation. Key off-page SEO strategies include:

1. Link building: Acquire high-quality, relevant backlinks from authoritative websites to boost your site's credibility in the eyes of search engines. Focus on creating valuable, shareable content to naturally attract backlinks.

2. Social media marketing: Actively promote your content on social media platforms to increase its visibility and reach. Social signals, such as likes, shares, and comments, can

contribute to your site's perceived authority.

3. Online directories and local citations: Submit your business information to reputable online directories and maintain consistent NAP (name, address, phone number) information to improve local search rankings.

4. Guest posting: Contribute high-quality content to reputable websites within your industry. This not only helps you acquire valuable backlinks but also positions you as an expert in your field.

By mastering both on-page and off-page SEO techniques, you can significantly enhance your brand's visibility in search results, drive more organic traffic to your website, and ultimately strengthen your online brand presence.

Maximizing the Impact of Customer Success Stories and Case Studies

While online reviews and testimonials are essential for building trust and credibility, going one step further by showcasing customer success stories and case studies can significantly enhance your online brand presence. These in-depth accounts of how your products or services have positively impacted customers can serve as powerful marketing tools, setting you apart from competitors and demonstrating real-world results.

1. Collect Customer Success Stories: Actively seek out satisfied customers who are willing to share their experiences with your product or service. Conduct interviews or ask them to fill out a questionnaire detailing the challenges they faced, the solutions you provided, and the results they achieved.

2. Create Compelling Case Studies: Transform these customer success stories into well-structured, engaging case studies. Include relevant data, statistics, and visuals to illustrate the impact of your product or service on your customers' businesses or lives.

3. Showcase Success Stories on Your Website: Dedicate a section of your website to displaying customer success stories and case studies. Organize them by industry or

solution type, making it easy for potential customers to find relatable examples that resonate with their specific needs.

4. Promote Success Stories on Social Media: Share these success stories and case studies on your social media profiles to reach a wider audience. Use eye-catching visuals and pull quotes to entice users to read the full story and learn more about the value your business offers.

5. Incorporate Customer Success Stories into Sales and Marketing Collateral: Include customer success stories in your sales presentations, marketing materials, and email campaigns. This provides social proof that your product or service delivers real-world results and helps potential

customers envision the benefits they could experience.

By focusing on customer success stories and case studies, you can provide a more comprehensive and convincing portrayal of your brand's value. This approach not only builds trust and credibility but also demonstrates the tangible, positive impact your business has on its customers, ultimately strengthening your online brand presence.

[3 Key Takeaways]

- Consistency and Professionalism: A strong online brand presence is built on a foundation of consistent branding and a professional website. Ensuring that your brand's visual elements, messaging, and website design are cohesive and polished will create a memorable and trustworthy image for your audience.

- Engagement and Value: Engaging with your audience on social media and providing them with valuable content are key factors in establishing credibility and trust. By creating tailored content and actively participating in relevant conversations, you can forge strong connections with your target audience and showcase your brand's expertise.

- Visibility and Social Proof: Mastering SEO and leveraging online reviews, testimonials, success stories, and case studies are crucial for increasing your brand's visibility and reinforcing its reputation. By optimizing your online presence for search engines and showcasing positive customer experiences, you can attract more potential customers and solidify your brand's position in the market.

Chapter 3: Amplify Your Brand's Impact Through Strategic Partnerships and Influencer Marketing

Building Strategic Partnerships and Collaborations for Local Businesses Across Various Industries

Local businesses across various industries can benefit significantly from building strategic partnerships and collaborating with influencers within their communities. In this chapter, we will discuss how businesses can leverage these strategies to enhance their brand awareness, credibility, and reach within their target market, both online and offline.

Forming Strategic Partnerships with Local Businesses:

- Identify complementary businesses: Look for local businesses that share your target audience but offer different products or services. For example, a fitness center might partner with a health food store, while an accountant could collaborate with a local attorney.

- Collaborate on joint promotions: Organize special events, discounts, or offers that benefit both parties, such as a health and wellness fair or a joint seminar on financial and legal planning.

- Share resources and expertise: Exchange knowledge, contacts, or resources with your partners to help each other grow and improve. This could involve sharing marketing tips, referring clients to each other, or offering joint training sessions.

Collaborating with Local Influencers:

- Identify relevant influencers: Look for local influencers or micro-influencers who have a strong presence in your community and share your target audience. For a fitness center, this might be a local fitness coach, while an accountant might connect with a financial planning influencer.
- Offer exclusive deals or experiences: Provide influencers with special offers, such as a free membership trial or discounted consultation, in

exchange for a review or promotion on their social media platforms.

- Host influencer events: Organize exclusive events for local influencers to experience your products or services firsthand, such as a workout challenge or a financial planning workshop.

Building Partnerships with Local Organizations and Events:

- Sponsor local events or charities: Support local events, fundraisers, or charities by sponsoring or donating your products or services. This not only showcases your commitment to the community but also increases your brand visibility.

- Collaborate with local organizations: Partner with local business associations, chambers of commerce, or community organizations to co-host events, seminars, or workshops that benefit your target audience.

By utilizing these strategies, local businesses across various industries can effectively amplify their brand's impact, strengthen their presence within the community, and foster long-lasting relationships with partners and influencers. These collaborative efforts can help local businesses expand their reach and drive growth in a competitive market, both online and offline.

[3 Key Takeaways]

1. Form strategic partnerships with complementary local businesses to pool resources, expertise, and customer bases, increasing brand exposure and credibility within the community.
2. Collaborate with local influencers to promote your products or services to a wider audience and leverage their credibility to attract new customers.
3. Engage with local organizations and events to demonstrate your commitment to the community, increase brand visibility, and establish valuable connections with potential customers and partners.

Part 2: Ideas for Various Business Types: (If your business type isn't listed reach out to us and we can help you)

In this section, we will explore how businesses of different types can utilize strategic partnerships and influencer marketing to enhance their branding and improve their online reputation.

Retail Businesses:

For retail businesses partnerships can be established with complementary brands to offer exclusive discounts, bundle deals, or limited-edition products. Collaborate with influencers who have a following that matches your target demographic to showcase your products and generate buzz.

Service Providers:

Service providers, such as accounting firms, legal services, or marketing agencies, can partner with other businesses to offer value-added services to their clients. Influencers with expertise in specific niches can help promote the service provider's expertise and credibility by endorsing their services and sharing testimonials.

Events and Hospitality:

Hotels, event venues, and restaurants can partner with local attractions, transportation services, or tour operators to create comprehensive packages for guests. Collaborate with influencers who have a strong following in the travel and lifestyle sectors to showcase your offerings and attract new customers.

Health and Wellness:

Health and wellness businesses, such as gyms, yoga studios, or nutrition coaches, can collaborate with complementary service providers, like physiotherapists or personal trainers, to provide a holistic approach to wellness. Partner with influencers who have a dedicated health-conscious following to promote your services and share their experiences.

Non-Profit Organizations:

Non-profits can partner with businesses or other non-profits to raise awareness for their cause, organize fundraising events, or pool resources to achieve common goals. Engage with influencers who have a passion for your cause to help amplify your message and reach a wider audience.

Online Businesses:

Online businesses can partner with complementary brands to offer exclusive deals, co-branded products, or affiliate marketing opportunities. Work with influencers to create content featuring your products or services, such as tutorials, reviews, or unboxing videos, to drive traffic to your website and increase conversions. In conclusion, strategic partnerships and influencer marketing can be effectively utilized by various types of businesses to enhance their branding and improve their online reputation. By identifying the right partners and influencers and tailoring your approach based on your business type, you can amplify your brand's impact and achieve your goals.

[3 Key Takeaways]

1. Understand your business type and identify potential partners and influencers who can help enhance your brand visibility and credibility.
2. Develop tailored campaigns and collaborations that leverage the unique strengths of your partners and influencers to promote your products or services.
3. Measure the success of your partnerships and influencer marketing efforts to continuously improve your strategy and achieve better results.

Chapter 4: **Tackle Negative Reviews and Navigate Online Reputation Crises with Confidence: Top Strategies for Success**

What are the best strategies for handling negative reviews and addressing online reputation crises?

Negative reviews and online reputation crises can pose significant challenges for businesses and individuals alike. In this chapter, we will discuss the best strategies for effectively handling negative reviews and addressing online reputation crises in a proactive and professional manner.

Monitor your online presence:

Monitoring your online presence is crucial to staying on top of your brand's reputation. Regularly monitoring review sites, social media profiles, and search engine results can help you identify any negative reviews or content as early as possible. This allows you to address the issue promptly and prevent any potential damage to your reputation.

One way to stay informed about new mentions or reviews is by setting up alerts using tools like Google Alerts, Mention, or specialized review monitoring platforms. These tools will notify you via email or dashboard alerts when new content mentioning your brand appears online. By being aware of any new mentions or reviews, you can respond in a timely and appropriate manner.

It's important to remember that monitoring your online presence is not just about addressing negative reviews or content. It's also about identifying positive feedback and leveraging it to enhance your reputation. By monitoring your brand's online presence, you can also identify areas where you can improve and adjust your strategy accordingly.

Overall, monitoring your online presence is an ongoing process that requires time and attention. But by staying on top of your brand's reputation, you can maintain a positive image and build trust with your audience.

Respond promptly and professionally:

Responding promptly and professionally to negative reviews is essential for maintaining a positive online reputation. By acknowledging and addressing the issue, businesses can show their commitment to customer satisfaction and demonstrate their willingness to improve.

When responding to negative reviews, it's important to remain calm and avoid becoming defensive. Start by acknowledging the reviewer's concerns and thanking them for their feedback. Apologize if necessary, and provide a clear course of action to resolve the issue.

If possible, move the conversation offline and provide contact information for the reviewer to discuss the issue in more detail. This not only helps to address the issue more effectively but also shows other potential customers that you take feedback seriously and are committed to resolving any issues.

It's also important to keep your responses professional and avoid personal attacks or negative language. Remember that your response is a reflection of your brand, and professionalism can go a long way in building trust with your audience.

In summary, responding promptly and professionally to negative reviews can help businesses demonstrate their commitment to customer satisfaction and improve their online reputation. By acknowledging the issue, providing a clear course of action, and remaining professional, businesses can effectively manage negative feedback and turn it into an opportunity for improvement.

Take the conversation offline:

Taking the conversation offline is a crucial strategy when addressing negative reviews or feedback. Engaging with the reviewer privately allows for a more personal and productive conversation, which can lead to a more positive outcome. When possible, provide the reviewer with an email address, phone number, or direct message to facilitate the conversation.

By moving the conversation away from public forums, you can avoid further negative exposure and demonstrate to the reviewer that you are taking their concerns seriously. This also provides an opportunity to gather more detailed feedback and address any underlying issues that may be impacting your business.

When engaging with the reviewer, be sure to approach the conversation in a professional and empathetic manner. Listen to their concerns, acknowledge their perspective, and provide a clear course of action to resolve the issue. By doing so, you can turn a negative experience into a positive one and demonstrate your commitment to excellent customer service.

Learn from negative feedback:

Negative feedback can be an invaluable tool for improving your business practices and enhancing your reputation. Rather than simply dismissing or ignoring negative feedback, take the time to carefully evaluate and analyze it to identify areas for improvement.

Start by identifying any patterns or common themes that emerge across multiple negative reviews or feedback. This could involve issues with a specific product or service, common complaints about customer service or communication, or other recurring themes.

Once you have identified these patterns, take steps to address them and implement changes that will prevent similar complaints from arising in the future. This could involve improving training for staff, updating products or services, or changing your communication or customer service processes.

It's important to also communicate these changes to your customers and publicly acknowledge that you have taken their feedback into account and are actively working to improve. By demonstrating your commitment to continuous improvement, you can not only address the specific concerns raised by negative feedback but also build trust and credibility with your audience.

Encourage positive reviews:

Encouraging positive reviews from satisfied customers can be a powerful way to enhance your online reputation. One effective strategy is to make it easy for customers to leave reviews by providing direct links or instructions on how to leave a review on relevant platforms such as Google, Facebook, or industry-specific review sites.

Additionally, businesses can incentivize customers to leave reviews by offering rewards or discounts for their feedback. This can be a great way to generate positive reviews and build customer loyalty.

Another way to encourage positive reviews is by providing outstanding customer service and asking for feedback after a positive experience. By demonstrating a commitment to customer satisfaction, businesses can create a culture of positivity that encourages customers to leave positive reviews.

Tools like Rep Master can also be incredibly helpful in encouraging positive reviews. With features like custom review pages and automated review streams, businesses can easily showcase their positive reviews and make it simple for customers to leave feedback. This can help to balance out any negative reviews and create a more accurate representation of the business's overall reputation.

It's important to remember that while positive reviews are valuable, businesses should never solicit or incentivize fake reviews. This can have severe consequences for their online reputation and credibility. Encouraging genuine, authentic feedback from satisfied customers is the best way to build a positive online reputation.

Be transparent and accountable:

When it comes to addressing an online reputation crisis or negative feedback, being transparent and accountable is crucial. Communicating openly with your audience and taking responsibility for any shortcomings shows customers that their concerns are being taken seriously and that steps are being taken to resolve the issue. This can help rebuild trust and repair your reputation.

Businesses can facilitate transparency and accountability by utilizing a review management platform, such as one that helps monitor their online reputation and respond promptly to any negative feedback. With such a platform, businesses can provide a clear course of action to resolve the issue and take the conversation offline if necessary.

Encouraging positive reviews is another way to mitigate the impact of negative reviews or crises. Businesses can streamline the review process for satisfied customers, creating a more accurate representation of their overall reputation. While tools like Rep Master can help facilitate this process, it's important to maintain transparency and accountability throughout the process to build and maintain a positive online reputation.

Transparency and accountability are critical components of managing and improving your online reputation. By utilizing tools like review management platforms and encouraging positive reviews, businesses can mitigate the impact of negative reviews or crises and maintain a positive reputation with their audience.

Monitor and adjust:

Monitoring and adjusting your approach is crucial to maintaining a positive online reputation in the long term. Even after addressing negative reviews or reputation crises, it's important to keep a close eye on your online presence and gather feedback from your audience. This allows you to identify any lingering issues and ensure that your reputation remains intact.

By regularly monitoring your online presence and analyzing feedback from customers, you can identify patterns and areas for improvement. Adjust your approach as needed to address any recurring issues and prevent future negative reviews or crises.

Tools like Rep Master can make this process easier by providing businesses with real-time alerts and analytics to track their online reputation. By utilizing such tools, businesses can stay ahead of potential issues and make informed decisions about how to improve their reputation.

In conclusion, managing your online reputation is an ongoing process that requires a commitment to continuous improvement. By regularly monitoring and adjusting your approach, businesses and individuals can successfully navigate negative reviews and reputation crises, and maintain a positive online reputation over the long term.

[3 Key Takeaways]

- Respond promptly and professionally to negative reviews, taking the conversation offline when possible, and use the feedback as an opportunity for improvement.

- Develop a crisis management plan to prepare for potential online reputation crises and ensure a coordinated, transparent, and accountable response.
- Proactively monitor your online presence, encourage positive reviews, and continually adjust your approach to maintain a positive reputation in the face of challenges.

Chapter 5: **Measure Your Online Reputation Management and Branding Triumphs: The Ultimate Guide to Assessing Your Digital Impact**

How can businesses and individuals measure the success of their online reputation management and branding efforts?

Measuring the success of online reputation management and branding efforts is crucial for businesses and individuals to evaluate the effectiveness of their strategies and make data-driven decisions for improvement. In this chapter, we will explore various methods and metrics to assess the success of online reputation management and branding initiatives.

Monitor online reviews and ratings:

Monitoring online reviews and ratings is essential for businesses to understand how their customers perceive their brand and the quality of their products or services. Regularly tracking the number and quality of reviews on platforms like Google, Yelp, and industry-specific sites can help businesses identify areas where they need to improve and adjust their reputation management efforts accordingly.

In addition to assessing the overall sentiment and average rating, analyzing trends in feedback can provide valuable insights into the effectiveness of reputation management efforts over time. This can help businesses identify patterns and make data-driven decisions to improve their online reputation.

Utilizing a review management platform can make it easier for businesses to monitor their online reviews and ratings across multiple platforms. Such a platform can provide a unified view of all the reviews and ratings in one place, making it easier to track trends and assess the overall sentiment.

Furthermore, a review management platform can help businesses quickly respond to negative reviews and mitigate the impact of any negative feedback. By responding promptly and professionally, businesses can show their customers that they care about their feedback and are committed to addressing any issues.

Overall, regularly monitoring online reviews and ratings is crucial for businesses to maintain a positive online reputation. By using a review management platform like Rep Master, businesses can streamline their reputation management efforts and stay on top of their online presence without having to manually check multiple platforms.

Analyze website metrics:

Analyzing website metrics is crucial for businesses to assess the effectiveness of their online branding efforts. By monitoring metrics such as the number of unique visitors, bounce rate, time on site, and conversion rate, businesses can identify areas for improvement and make data-driven decisions to optimize their website.

One useful tool for tracking website metrics is Google Analytics, which provides detailed insights into user behavior and engagement on your site. With Google Analytics, businesses can track key performance indicators such as page views, sessions, and goal completions. They can also segment their audience by demographics, geography, and behavior to gain a better understanding of their target market.

Analyzing website metrics can help businesses identify areas for improvement, such as optimizing page load times, improving navigation and usability, or adjusting website content to better align with customer interests and preferences. By making these improvements, businesses can enhance the user experience, increase engagement, and ultimately drive more conversions and revenue.

While there are many tools and platforms available to help businesses track website metrics, it's important to choose the ones that align with your specific goals and objectives. By regularly monitoring and analyzing website metrics, businesses can optimize their online branding efforts and ensure they are achieving the desired results.

Evaluate social media performance:

Evaluating social media performance is essential for businesses and individuals to determine the effectiveness of their social media marketing efforts. Social media platforms offer various analytics tools to track metrics such as the number of followers, engagement rate, reach, and conversions.

The number of followers on social media can indicate the size of your audience and the potential reach of your content. However, it's also important to track engagement metrics, such as likes, comments, and shares, to assess the level of interest and interaction from your audience. The reach of your content, or the number of people who see your posts, is another critical metric to monitor.

Conversion metrics, such as click-through rates and lead generation, can provide insights into the effectiveness of your social media strategies in driving traffic and sales.

It's essential to use platform-specific analytics tools, such as Facebook Insights or Twitter Analytics, to gather data and assess the success of your social media campaigns.

Overall, evaluating social media performance can help businesses and individuals identify which strategies and tactics are most effective in engaging their audience and driving results. By regularly tracking these metrics, you can make data-driven decisions and improve your social media marketing efforts over time.

Assess search engine rankings:

Assessing your search engine rankings is another important aspect of measuring the success of your online reputation management and branding efforts. By monitoring your rankings for relevant keywords and phrases, you can determine how visible your business or personal brand is online, as well as the effectiveness of your SEO strategy.

Tools like Google Search Console, AHREFS, or SEMrush can provide valuable insights into your search engine performance. With these tools, you can track your search engine rankings over time, identify opportunities for improvement, and adjust your SEO strategy accordingly.

When assessing your search engine rankings, consider factors such as the keywords and phrases you are targeting, the competition in your industry or niche, and any changes to search engine algorithms that may impact your rankings.

Overall, monitoring and analyzing your search engine rankings is a crucial component of assessing the success of your online reputation management and branding efforts. By staying on top of your search engine performance, you can ensure that your brand is visible to your target audience and that your SEO efforts are contributing to the growth and success of your business or personal brand.

Measure brand awareness and sentiment:

Measuring brand awareness and sentiment is essential for evaluating the success of branding efforts. Surveys, social listening platforms, and sentiment analysis software

are effective tools to gauge brand awareness and sentiment among your target audience.

Surveys can provide direct feedback from customers and potential customers, allowing you to assess the effectiveness of your branding efforts and identify areas for improvement. Social listening platforms allow you to track brand mentions and conversations on social media and other online platforms, giving you valuable insights into the sentiment surrounding your brand.

Sentiment analysis software uses natural language processing and machine learning algorithms to analyze the sentiment of online mentions and reviews of your brand. This can help you identify patterns in the feedback and make data-driven decisions for improving your brand's reputation.

While there are many tools available for measuring brand awareness and sentiment, it's important to choose the ones that align with your specific goals and target audience. By regularly measuring and analyzing brand awareness and sentiment, businesses and individuals can make informed decisions for improving their branding efforts and building a positive reputation online.

Track customer satisfaction and loyalty:

Tracking customer satisfaction and loyalty is a crucial aspect of evaluating the success of your reputation management and branding initiatives. Metrics such as Net

Promoter Score (NPS), customer retention rate, and customer lifetime value (CLV) can provide valuable insights into the effectiveness of your strategies in fostering long-term relationships with your customers.

Net Promoter Score (NPS) measures customer loyalty and satisfaction by asking customers to rate on a scale of 0-10 how likely they are to recommend your business to others. The scores are categorized into Promoters (9-10), Passives (7-8), and Detractors (0-6). By calculating the percentage of Promoters minus Detractors, you can determine your overall NPS and identify areas for improvement.

Customer retention rate measures the percentage of customers who continue to do business with you over time. A high retention rate indicates that your customers are satisfied with your products or services and are likely to continue doing business with you.

Customer lifetime value (CLV) measures the total amount of revenue a customer is expected to generate over the course of their relationship with your business. By tracking CLV, you can identify which customers are the most valuable to your business and tailor your marketing and customer service strategies accordingly.

By tracking these metrics, businesses and individuals can evaluate the success of their reputation management and branding efforts in building and maintaining customer satisfaction and loyalty. Additionally, these metrics can provide insights into areas for improvement and help to inform future strategies for long-term success.

Calculate return on investment (ROI):

Calculating the return on investment (ROI) of your online reputation management and branding efforts is essential to ensure that your strategies are generating a positive impact on your business. To calculate your ROI, you need to compare the costs of your initiatives with the revenue generated from increased brand visibility, customer acquisition, and customer retention.

First, you need to identify the costs associated with your reputation management and branding initiatives, such as the cost of tools and software, advertising costs, and personnel expenses. Next, you need to track the revenue generated from these initiatives, such as the revenue generated from new customer acquisitions, repeat customers, and upselling.

To calculate your ROI, you can use the following formula:

ROI = (Revenue - Cost) / Cost x 100%

For example, if you spent $10,000 on your reputation management and branding efforts and generated $20,000 in revenue, your ROI would be:

ROI = ($20,000 - $10,000) / $10,000 x 100% = 100%

This means that for every dollar spent on your reputation management and branding efforts, you generated $2 in revenue.

Measuring ROI is crucial to identify the effectiveness of your initiatives and optimize your strategies for maximum impact. Utilizing tools like Rep Master can help businesses monitor their online reputation and track the success of their initiatives to ensure a positive ROI.

To sum up, it is essential for businesses and individuals to measure the success of their online reputation management and branding efforts through a combination of quantitative and qualitative metrics. This includes regularly tracking and analyzing website metrics, social media performance, search engine rankings, brand awareness and sentiment, customer satisfaction and loyalty, and return on investment. By doing so, they can evaluate the effectiveness of their strategies, identify areas for improvement, and make informed decisions for future success.

[3 Key Takeaways]

- Assess the success of your online reputation management and branding efforts using a combination of metrics, such as online reviews, website analytics, social media performance, and search engine rankings.
- Monitor brand awareness and sentiment among your target audience using surveys, social

listening platforms, and sentiment analysis tools to identify areas for improvement.

- Measure customer satisfaction, loyalty, and return on investment to evaluate the long-term impact of your reputation management and branding initiatives.

Chapter 6: **The Holistic Approach to Online Reputation Mastery: Integrating Strategies and Embracing the Ultimate Solution**

In the previous chapters, we've explored the various facets of online reputation management and branding. From mastering the art of building and managing your online reputation to leveraging social media platforms and handling negative reviews, each aspect plays a crucial role in your digital success. Now, it's time to bring everything together and introduce an all-encompassing solution that can help you achieve your online reputation and branding goals seamlessly.

The Integrated Approach: Why Tying Everything Together Matters

Building a strong online presence requires a holistic approach that combines all the strategies we've discussed so far. By integrating these tactics, you'll create a cohesive and comprehensive digital footprint that attracts customers, enhances your brand image, and fosters long-term success. A powerful all-in-one solution can help you manage every aspect of your online reputation and branding, making it easier than ever to implement the strategies we've covered.

The Ultimate Online Reputation and Branding Solution

A robust online reputation management solution streamlines the entire process of managing your online reputation and building a powerful brand presence. With features like automatic review monitoring, custom review and survey pages, ready-to-use text and email sequences, and employee training tools, your business will be empowered to take control of its digital destiny.

Harnessing the Power of an All-in-One Solution to Maximize Your Digital Domination

By incorporating a comprehensive solution into your online reputation management and branding strategy, you'll unlock the full potential of the techniques we've discussed in this book. A powerful platform not only simplifies the process but also helps you stay on top of your online reputation, ensuring you never miss an opportunity to improve your digital presence.

Continuous Improvement: The Road to Unstoppable Business Success

As with any aspect of your business, mastering your online reputation and branding is an ongoing process that requires constant attention and adaptation. With a powerful all-in-one solution by your side, you can be confident that you have the tools and support you need to navigate the ever-evolving digital landscape and achieve long-lasting success.

By embracing the holistic approach to online reputation management and branding, and utilizing the powerful features of a comprehensive solution, your business will be poised to dominate the digital realm and enjoy unstoppable growth. Remember, your online reputation and brand presence are essential for success in today's competitive marketplace, so take control now and start building the digital empire you've always dreamed of.

Conclusion:

As we reach the end of this comprehensive guide to online reputation and branding, it is crucial to reflect on the key lessons and insights garnered throughout this journey. The digital landscape presents a wealth of opportunities for businesses and individuals to establish, enhance, and protect their online reputation and brand. However, it also brings its share of challenges that require a proactive, strategic approach to navigate successfully.

In this concluding chapter, we will recap some of the most important takeaways from the book and emphasize the significance of continuous learning and adaptation in the ever-evolving world of online reputation and branding.

Key Takeaways

Throughout this guide, we have explored various aspects of online reputation and branding, including:

- The importance of building and managing a strong online reputation for businesses and individuals
- The key elements that contribute to a compelling online brand presence
- The role of social media platforms in enhancing online reputation and branding efforts

- Strategies for handling negative reviews and addressing online reputation crises
- Methods for measuring the success of online reputation management and branding initiatives

By implementing the strategies and best practices outlined in these chapters, businesses and individuals can successfully navigate the challenges of the digital landscape and create a positive, impactful online reputation and brand.

The Importance of Continuous Learning and Adaptation

The digital world is constantly evolving, with new technologies, platforms, and trends emerging at a rapid pace. To maintain a strong online reputation and brand presence, it is essential to stay informed about these developments and adapt your strategies accordingly.

Continuously learning from your own experiences, as well as the successes and failures of others, can provide valuable insights that will help you refine your approach and stay ahead of the competition. Moreover, staying engaged with your audience, actively soliciting feedback, and being open to change will ensure that your online reputation and brand remain relevant and resonant in the ever-changing digital landscape.

Final Thoughts

In conclusion, the management of online reputation and branding has become a critical aspect of success in the digital age. By leveraging the expert insights, practical examples, and actionable strategies provided within this guide, businesses and individuals can harness the power of the internet to build a positive and impactful online reputation and brand.

Ultimately, the key to success lies in continuous learning, adaptation, and a commitment to excellence. By embracing these principles and applying the lessons learned throughout this book, you will be well-equipped to navigate the challenges and opportunities of the digital world and achieve your personal and professional goals.

Unlock the Secret to a Stellar Online Reputation and Branding Strategy

As a business owner or entrepreneur, you know that your online reputation and branding strategy can make or break your success. In today's digital landscape, it's more important than ever to have a strong, consistent online presence that reflects your values, expertise, and achievements. But, let's be honest – managing your online reputation and building a powerful brand presence can be daunting and time-consuming. That's where we come in! Introducing Rep Master, the ultimate online reputation and branding system designed to help businesses like yours thrive in the digital space. Developed by industry experts with years of experience in digital marketing and reputation management, Rep Master provides a comprehensive suite of tools and strategies that can take your online presence to new heights.

With Rep Master, you'll discover how to:

- Build and manage your online reputation effectively, ensuring your business stands out from the competition
- Craft a strong and consistent online brand presence that resonates with your target audience
- Leverage social media platforms to boost your online reputation and enhance your branding efforts
- Handle negative reviews and navigate online reputation crises with confidence

- Measure the success of your online reputation management and branding initiatives to ensure continuous improvement

But don't just take our word for it! See for yourself how Rep Master can revolutionize your online reputation and branding strategy.

Schedule a Free Demo Today at www.RepMaster.io

By taking the next step and scheduling a demo, you'll gain access to the powerful tools and expert guidance you need to elevate your online reputation and brand presence. Don't miss this opportunity to unlock the secret to a stellar digital presence and skyrocket your business success!

Remember, your online reputation and brand are the keys to your success in the digital world. Don't leave them to chance – let Rep Master help you unlock your full potential.

Take action now and experience the transformative power of Rep Master. Visit the URL below to schedule your demo and embark on the journey to a stronger, more impactful online presence.

www.RepMaster.io

We look forward to helping you achieve your digital marketing goals and building a lasting partnership that leads to success.

Sincerely,
Brian Carson
Founder RepMaster.io

About The Author:

Brian Carson, a seasoned digital marketing professional and proud owner of Bash Web Consulting, has spent the past decade mastering the art of online reputation management and helping businesses thrive in the digital space. As a former athlete and a firm believer in hard work, ethics, and helping others, Brian's journey is one of resilience, determination, and success.

Growing up in challenging circumstances, Brian learned the value of hard work and perseverance from a young age. After excelling in sports and pursuing higher education, he took on a series of jobs to support his family. Through unwavering determination, Brian went back to school to earn a bachelor's degree in business management and eventually started his own business.

Today, Bash Web Consulting is a respected boutique-style digital marketing agency that has built long-lasting relationships with clients. With a 98% client retention rate, Brian's commitment to client success and personalized support has earned him a reputation for excellence.

As a certified email marketing specialist and has been mentored by the best SEOs and Media Buyers in the world, Brian brings a wealth of expertise and experience to his work. Having worked with a diverse range of businesses, from construction to children's party services, Brian's understanding of the importance of online presence led him to specialize in SEO, website design and affiliate marketing.

Brian's personal values and professional principles are deeply ingrained in the company culture at Bash Web Consulting and Rep Master. This dedication to quality service and client success has made him a trusted partner to businesses seeking to enhance their online reputation and achieve digital marketing success.

In this book, Brian shares his knowledge and insights, providing readers with invaluable strategies for building and managing their online reputation, crafting a strong brand presence, and leveraging digital platforms to achieve their goals.

www.ingramcontent.com/pod-product-compliance
Lightning Source LLC
Chambersburg PA
CBHW071136220526
45467CB00015B/1185